THE LITTLE
SALAD
COOKBOOK

THE LITTLE
SALAD
COOKBOOK

SMITHMARK

This edition first published in 1996 by
SMITHMARK Publishers
a division of US Media Holdings Inc.
16 East 32nd Street
New York, NY 10016

Produced by Anness Publishing Limited
1 Boundary Row
London SE1 8HP

SMITHMARK books are available for bulk purchase for
sales promotion and for premium use. For details write or
call the manager of special sales, SMITHMARK
Publishers, a division of US Media Holdings Inc., 16 East
32nd Street, New York, NY 10016; (212 532 6600)

ISBN 0-8317-7380-4

Publisher Joanna Lorenz
Senior Cookery Editor Linda Fraser
Assistant Editor Emma Brown
Designers Patrick McLeavey & Jo Brewer
Illustrator Anna Koska
Photographers Karl Adamson, Michael Michaels,
James Duncan, Steve Baxter, Amanda Heywood
& Edward Allwright
Recipes Christine France, Roz Denny, Catherine Atkinson,
Hilaire Walden, Steven Wheeler, Annie Nichols,
Shirley Gill & Norma MacMillan

10 9 8 7 6 5 4 3 2 1

Printed in Singapore by
Star Standard Industries Pte Ltd

Contents

Introduction

Thanks to the abundance of good quality salad-stuffs in our grocery stores, these once seasonal treats can now be enjoyed every day. It is true that there's a special pleasure in gathering greens and fresh herbs from the garden, but when summer gives way to fall, and even the cut-and-come again lettuces no longer yield fresh young leaves, it is satisfying to know that salads can still be on the menu.

There's no better way to exercise artistic flair than in assembling a salad. Even a simple green salad can offer subtle variations in shape, texture, color and flavor. Contrast a crisphead lettuce with a soft leaf lettuce; the long elegant leaves of a Romaine with the matt glossy green of spinach. Balance bland flavors with a few leaves of bitter escarole, or introduce an underlying lemon flavor with some shreds of sorrel. Nasturtium leaves add a peppery tang, as does arugula, while young spinach leaves are valued for their rich sweetness. For extra color, choose the red or purple hues of oakleaf lettuce or red cabbage, perhaps accentuated by a few feathery leaves from the heart of a frisée lettuce. Take care not to overdo it; two or three different types of greens, chosen for their complementary or contrasting qualities, will be more effective than an ill-assorted medley.

As for extra ingredients, the list is almost endless. Salad vegetables include avocados, artichokes, asparagus, green beans, carrots, cauliflower florets, celery, cucumber, fennel, bell peppers of every color, radishes and onions, especially Spanish or mild red onions. Tomatoes too, although these are often served on their own, with a simple olive oil dressing and snippings of basil. Vinegar is seldom added because tomatoes are themselves acidic. Fruits, especially oranges, apples, pears, grapes and melons, frequently feature in salads.

Potato salads are in a category of their own, and there are also many hearty salads based on rice, pasta or grains, including the Middle-Eastern tabbouleh. Meats, fish and shellfish make a major contribution.

It is traditional to serve a simple salad after the main course, but a salad can serve equally well as an appetizer, accompaniment or substantial main course.

Salads were originally seasoned solely with salt (hence the name) but are now inseparably associated with a whole host of dressings, from simple mixtures of oil and vinegar or lemon juice to sauces based on mayonnaise, yogurt or blue cheese. Hot dressings, often with a foundation of bacon fat (the crisp fried bacon giving the salad extra flavor and texture) are increasingly popular, but must be added only at the last minute; if either dinner or diner is late, the leaves will become limp and the salad will be spoiled.

We are constantly being encouraged to eat more fresh vegetables and fruit. What better way to enjoy these ingredients than in a salad that is as pleasing to look at and to make as it is delicious to eat?

7

Familiar Salad Leaves

BUTTERHEAD LETTUCE
Named after its soft, buttery-textured leaves. This lettuce is sweet and succulent. Boston and Bibb are the most well known.

CHINESE CABBAGE
Two types of this crunchy vegetable are commonly seen; one is longer and more pointed than the other. Both have delicately flavored long, crinkly leaves with crisp, white stems. It is available all year round and keeps well in the refrigerator.

ROMAINE LETTUCE
Firm, tapering leaves with a stiff central rib, tightly packed to form an elongated head, the romaine or Cos lettuce is one of the most familiar and is the lettuce of choice for caesar salads.

ENDIVE
There are several varieties of this loose-leaved salad vegetable: Batavian endive (escarole) has broad, ragged leaves, while the leaves of curly endive (frisée) are frilly, almost spiky. A red broad-leafed variety, radicchio, is favored for its color and texture. All endives tend to be rather bitter.

CRISPHEAD LETTUCE
With its large, firm head and tightly packed, crisp leaves, this is one of the most popular varieties of lettuce. It keeps for longer than most lettuces.

CORN SALAD
Also known as lamb's lettuce or mâche, corn salad consists of small, smooth, green leaves in clusters. The leaves have a mild, sweet flavor. It is preferable to buy corn salad loose in whole plants, since it is fragile and bruises easily.

RED LEAF

One of the most popular leaf lettuces, with pretty frilly leaves that are dark green near the stalk and red-tinged at the outer edges.

GREEN LEAF

Mild-tasting green leaf lettuces have distinctive, crinkly leaves forming a loose head. Depending on the variety, green leaf lettuces can range from pale to dark green.

OAKLEAF LETTUCE

Also known as feuille de chêne and red salad bowl, this lettuce is favored for its color (bronze to purple) and its delicate flavor. It has loose leaves branching from a single stalk.

ARUGULA

This easy-to-grow, old-fashioned salad herb rewards gardeners with irregular, small, dark leaves which have a peppery flavor with a hint of citrus.

SALAD CRESS

Cress is bought growing in small trays or boxes; one simply snips off what is needed. It is a popular and pretty salad ingredient.

SORREL

The leaves of this herb, available from specialty produce stores, have a delicate lemony taste. Use raw sorrel sparingly. It does not keep well and must be bought fresh.

SPINACH

Tender young spinach leaves have a sweet flavor and are delicious with bacon.

WATERCRESS

Watercress leaves are dark and glossy and grow on sprigged stems. Watercress is a member of the mustard family, as one might suppose from its peppery flavor.

9

Techniques

CHOOSING SALAD GREENS

For the best flavor and texture, salad leaves must be fresh. Reject any that are wilted or discolored. Buy or pick only what you can use within the next day or two, and store them in the refrigerator.

PREPARING SALAD GREENS

To prepare lettuces, remove the coarse outer leaves, separate the remaining leaves and wash them well. Take care to remove any grit, but do not leave them to soak. Drain well, break off any tough ribs and dry the leaves. Use a salad spinner for the more robust leaves; blot delicate leaves with paper towels or a clean absorbent towel. If you must prepare lettuces ahead of time, pack the leaves into plastic bags, close tightly and store in the refrigerator.

MAKING A SIMPLE DRESSING

Dressings should be carefully chosen in order to complement the ingredients, and should not dominate the salad. A wide range of recipes appears in this collection, but for a simple French dressing the rule of thumb is to use three parts of olive oil to one part of wine vinegar, adding a pinch each of sugar, salt and pepper, and mustard powder or made mustard, for flavoring. Either combine all the ingredients in a screw-top jar, close tightly and shake well, or mix together the vinegar and the flavorings, then whisk in the oil.

10

TOSSING A GREEN SALAD

Rub the inside of the salad bowl with a cut clove of garlic, if you like. Just before serving, toss the greens with just enough dressing to coat them. It is better to err on the mean side than to swamp the salad.

TOPPINGS

- Crumbled crisp bacon or toasted nori (dried seaweed)
- Toasted sunflower, sesame or pumpkin seeds
- Snipped chives, chopped parsley or other fresh herbs
- Grated hard-boiled egg (white and yolk)
- Grated cheese
- Slivers of sun-dried tomato
- Cubes of feta cheese or smoked tofu

11

SPROUTING BEANS

Bean sprouts make a nutritious addition to a salad. Put the dried beans, seeds or grains (try mung beans, aduki beans or alfalfa seeds) in a large glass jar, filling it less than one-sixth full. Cover with cheesecloth secured by a rubber band, and fill the jar with cold water. Pour off the water and put the jar in a warm, dark spot. Rinse and drain daily. The sprouts will be ready to harvest in 3–6 days, and should be rinsed and drained before use.

COOK'S TIP

The best way to prepare a crisphead lettuce is to remove the core, then hold the head under running cold water to fill the cavity. The water will gently force the leaves apart, making it easy to remove as many as you need. Discard any outer leaves that are limp or have been torn or bruised.

Appetizers & Light Meals

Pear & Pecan Salad with Blue Cheese Dressing

INGREDIENTS

¾ cup shelled pecan nuts,
roughly chopped
3 crisp dessert pears
6 ounces young spinach, leaves stripped
from stems
1 escarole or butterhead lettuce, separated
into leaves
1 radicchio, separated into leaves
salt and ground black pepper
warm crusty bread, to serve
BLUE CHEESE DRESSING
1 ounce blue cheese, crumbled
3 tablespoons natural yogurt
2 teaspoons lemon juice
1 tablespoon olive oil
1 teaspoon snipped chives

SERVES 6

1 Make the dressing. Combine the cheese, yogurt and lemon juice in a small bowl. Gradually add the olive oil, beating constantly. Stir in the chives and add salt and pepper to taste. Preheat the broiler.

2 Spread out the pecans on a baking sheet. Toast under the broiler until golden, taking care not to allow them to scorch. Cut the unpeeled pears into quarters. Carefully remove the cores, then cut each pear quarter into thin even slices.

3 Mix the salad greens, and pears in a bowl. Add 2 tablespoons of the dressing and toss lightly until the leaves are coated. Season. Divide among six plates,

scatter over the pecan nuts and serve with crusty bread. Offer the remaining dressing separately.

Lobster Salad

INGREDIENTS

1 or 2 medium cooked lobsters
1½ pounds new potatoes, scrubbed
4 oranges
*7-ounce can young artichokes in brine, drained
and quartered*
4 tablespoons extra virgin olive oil
½ frisée lettuce, separated into leaves
6 ounces corn salad
2 tomatoes, peeled, seeded and diced
1 small bunch tarragon, chervil or Italian parsley
ORANGE BUTTER DRESSING
2 tablespoons orange juice
6 tablespoons butter, diced
salt and cayenne pepper

SERVES 4

1 Twist off the legs and claws from the lobster(s), and separate the tail piece from the body section. Break the claws open with a hammer and remove the meat in one piece. Use scissors to cut away the thin underside of the tail shell. Gently pull out the meat in one piece. Cut into slices and set aside.

2 Place the potatoes in a large saucepan of salted water. Bring to the boil, lower the heat slightly and cook for 15–20 minutes or until just tender. Drain and leave to cool.

3 Placing each orange in turn on a board, slice off the top and bottom neatly, taking care to remove all the pith. Using the same knife, cut off the peel on the sides of the orange, following the contours of the fruit. Then, holding the fruit over a bowl to catch the juice, slice very carefully between the membranes to remove the segments. Put the orange segments to one side. Remove the skin from the potatoes and cut them in half. Toss the orange segments, potatoes and artichokes lightly with a little of the olive oil.

4 Make the dressing. Place the orange juice in a heatproof bowl set over a pan of simmering water. Heat for 1 minute, then turn off the heat and whisk in the butter, a little at a time, until the dressing reaches a coating consistency. Add salt and a pinch of cayenne to taste. If necessary, thin the dressing with some of the fresh orange juice. Cover the dressing and keep it warm.

5 Toss the prepared salad leaves with some of the remaining olive oil in a bowl, then arrange them on four or six plates, depending on whether the salad is to be served as an appetizer or light meal. Following the illustration opposite, or a composition of your own, add the potatoes, artichokes, orange segments and lobster slices. Spoon the warm dressing over the top, add the tomato and garnish with the herbs. Serve at room temperature.

14

Tabbouleh

INGREDIENTS

⅔ cup bulgur
8 ounces tomatoes, peeled and seeded
1 small red onion, chopped
3 scallions, chopped
2 fat garlic cloves, crushed
1 cup finely chopped fresh parsley,
4 tablespoons chopped fresh mint
½ cup olive oil
5 tablespoons lemon juice
salt and ground black pepper
black olives and mint leaves, to garnish

SERVES 6

1 Place the bulgur in a strainer and rinse under cold running water until the water runs clear. Place in a bowl, cover with fresh cold water and leave to soak for 1 hour. Line the strainer with a clean dish towel, pour in the bulgur and drain thoroughly. Gather up the sides of the dish towel and squeeze well to remove all the excess moisture. Carefully tip the bulgur into a mixing bowl.

2 Cut the tomatoes into small dice. Stir into the drained bulgur in the bowl, with the onion, scallions, garlic, and parsley. Add the mint and mix well.

3 Whisk together the olive oil and lemon juice in a small bowl, and season. Pour this dressing over the salad. Toss gently so the dressing is absorbed. Taste, and add more salt, pepper and lemon juice if liked. Serve at room temperature, garnished with sliced black olives and whole mint leaves.

Minted Melon Salad

INGREDIENTS

1 ripe orange-fleshed melon
1 ripe green or white-fleshed melon
mint sprigs, to garnish
DRESSING
2 tablespoons roughly chopped fresh mint
1 teaspoon sugar
2 tablespoons raspberry vinegar
6 tablespoons extra virgin olive oil
salt and ground black pepper

SERVES 6

17

1 Cut the melons in half, then scoop out and discard the seeds. Using a sharp knife, cut the melons into thin slices. Carefully remove the skins. Take six individual salad plates and arrange slices of the two varieties of melon decoratively on each one.

2 Make the dressing. Mix together the mint, sugar and raspberry vinegar in a small bowl. Gradually whisk in the oil, then add salt and pepper to taste. Alternatively,

mix all the ingredients in a screw-top jar, close tightly and shake vigorously to combine.

3 Spoon the dressing over the melon slices. Serve lightly chilled and garnished with mint sprigs.

Eggplant & Bell Pepper Pâté with Radicchio

INGREDIENTS

1 radicchio, separated into leaves
1 butterhead lettuce, separated into leaves
crispbreads, to serve
PATE
3 eggplants
2 red bell peppers
5 garlic cloves
1½ teaspoons pink peppercorns in brine,
drained and crushed (optional)
2 tablespoons chopped fresh cilantro

SERVES 6

1 Make the pâté. Preheat the oven to 400°F. Arrange the eggplants, bell peppers and the unpeeled garlic cloves on a baking sheet. Bake for about 10 minutes, then remove the garlic cloves. Turn the vegetables over and bake for 20 minutes more. Peel the garlic and put into a food processor or blender.

2 Remove the charred bell peppers from the oven. Place in a plastic bag, close tightly and leave to cool. Bake the eggplants for a further 10 minutes.

3 Remove the eggplants from the oven, split them in half and scoop the flesh into a strainer placed over a bowl. Press the flesh with a spoon to remove the bitter juices, then add to the garlic. Process until smooth, then scrape into a large bowl.

4 Remove the bell peppers from the plastic bag and rub or peel off the skins and discard. Remove and discard the seeds, then chop the flesh finely. Stir the diced peppers into the eggplant and garlic mixture together with the pink peppercorns, if using, and the chopped fresh cilantro.

5 Choose a few radicchio and butterhead lettuce leaves of similar size and arrange them in an attractive pattern around the edges of six individual salad plates. Place a few spoonfuls of the eggplant and bell pepper pâté in the center of each plate of salad. Serve at once, with crispbreads, if liked.

18

Melon & Prosciutto Salad

INGREDIENTS

1 large melon (cantaloupe or Charentais)
6 ounces prosciutto, thinly sliced

SALSA

2 cups strawberries, hulled
1 teaspoon sugar
2 tablespoons peanut or sunflower oil
1 tablespoon orange juice
½ teaspoon finely grated orange rind
½ teaspoon finely grated fresh ginger
salt and ground black pepper

SERVES 4

1 Cut the melon in half and then scoop out and discard the seeds. Using a sharp knife, cut the melon into thick slices. Carefully remove the skin.

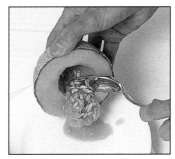

Place the slices on a plate in a single layer, cover and chill in the refrigerator until ready to serve.

2 Make the salsa. Cut the strawberries into large dice. Place them in a bowl with the sugar and crush lightly to release the juices. Add the oil, orange juice,

orange rind and ginger. Season with salt and a generous grinding of black pepper.

3 Arrange the melon on a serving plate and drape over the prosciutto. Serve with the strawberry salsa.

20

Smoked Trout & Horseradish Salad

INGREDIENTS

1½ pounds new potatoes, scrubbed
4 ounces mixed salad greens
4 smoked trout fillets, skinned and flaked
4 slices of dark rye bread, cut into small fingers
4 cherry tomatoes, halved
salt and ground black pepper
DRESSING
4 tablespoons horseradish cream
1 tablespoon white wine vinegar
4 tablespoons peanut oil
2 teaspoons caraway seeds

SERVES 4

1 Place the potatoes in a large pan of salted water. Bring to a boil, lower the heat slightly and cook for 15–20 minutes or until just tender. Drain and cool.

2 Make the dressing. Mix the horseradish and vinegar in a small bowl. Whisk in the oil. Stir in the caraway seeds. Alternatively, mix the ingredients in a screw-top jar, close tightly and shake to combine.

3 Put the prepared salad greens in a bowl. Season with salt and pepper and toss with a little of the dressing. Cut the potatoes in half. Arrange the trout, potatoes, rye fingers and cherry tomatoes on the salad, drizzle over a little more dressing and serve. Offer the remaining dressing separately.

Main Course Salads

New Orleans Steak Salad

INGREDIENTS

4 steaks, about 6 ounces each
1 butterhead lettuce, separated into leaves
1 bunch watercress, trimmed
4 tomatoes, quartered
4 drained canned artichoke hearts, halved
2¼ cups mushrooms, sliced
4 scallions, sliced
4 large gherkins, sliced
a few green olives
salt and ground black pepper
FRENCH DRESSING
1 tablespoon white wine vinegar
1 teaspoon Dijon mustard
pinch of sugar
6 tablespoons extra virgin olive oil

SERVES 4

I Lightly season the steaks with pepper. Place the steaks on a rack over a broiler pan and broil for about 6–8 minutes, turning once, until they are medium-rare. Cover the steaks with foil and leave in a warm place while you assemble the rest of the salad.

2 Make the dressing. Mix the vinegar, mustard and sugar in a small bowl, then whisk in the oil. Alternatively, mix all the ingredients in a screw-top jar, close tightly and shake to combine.

3 Put the lettuce, watercress, tomatoes, artichoke hearts and mushrooms in a bowl. Add the dressing and toss together lightly. Divide the salad among four plates and arrange the scallions, gherkins and olives on each. Slice each steak diagonally and arrange over the salads. Season with salt and pepper and serve at once.

23

Goat Cheese Salad with Buckwheat, Fresh Figs & Walnuts

INGREDIENTS

1 ½ cups couscous
2 tablespoons toasted buckwheat
2 tablespoons chopped fresh parsley
4 tablespoons olive oil
3 tablespoons walnut oil
4 cups arugula
½ frisée lettuce, separated into leaves
6 ounces crumbly white goat cheese
½ cup walnut pieces, toasted
4 ripe figs
salt and ground black pepper

SERVES 4

1 Mix the couscous and buckwheat together in a heatproof bowl. Pour over enough boiling water to cover and leave to soak for 15 minutes. Drain well in a strainer, then spread the mixture out on a metal tray and set aside to dry out a little more.

2 Tip the couscous mixture into a bowl. Add the chopped fresh parsley. Mix the olive oil and walnut oil together, then add half the dressing to the couscous mixture and toss lightly. Season to taste with salt and pepper.

3 Place the prepared arugula and frisée leaves in a separate bowl, add the remaining oil mixture and toss to coat. Arrange the dressed salad leaves on four large plates, especially around the edges, and pile couscous mixture in the center of each one.

4 Crumble or cube the goat cheese and arrange it over the salads, then scatter with the toasted walnut pieces. Using a sharp knife, carefully cut each fig into four from the top almost to the base. Leave the quarters joined at the base so that they open out like the petals of a flower. Gently center a fig on each salad and serve immediately.

24

Broiled Salmon & Spring Vegetable Salad

INGREDIENTS

12 ounces small new potatoes, scrubbed
4 quail's eggs
4 ounces baby zucchini, topped and tailed
4 ounces young carrots, peeled
4 ounces baby corn cobs
4 ounces sugar snap peas, trimmed
4 ounces fine green beans, trimmed
4 ounces pattypan squash (optional)
½ cup French dressing
4 salmon fillets, about 5 ounces each, skinned
4 cups sorrel or young spinach, leaves stripped
from stems
salt and ground black pepper

SERVES 4

1 Put the potatoes in a pan of salted water. Bring to a boil, lower the heat slightly and cook for 15–20 minutes or until just tender. Drain and keep warm.

2 Put the quail's eggs in a pan. Add boiling water to cover and simmer for 7–8 minutes. Cool under cold running water. Shell the eggs and cut them in half.

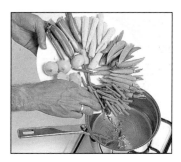

3 Peel the zucchini decoratively. Cook the carrots, corn, peas, beans, zucchini and squash (if using) in a pan of boiling water for about 2 minutes. Drain well and put in a bowl. Add the potatoes. Toss with a little French dressing, season and allow to cool. Preheat the broiler.

4 Put the salmon fillets on a rack over a broiler pan, brush with a little of the dressing and broil them for 6 minutes, turning once. Meanwhile, put the sorrel or spinach leaves in a stainless steel or enamel saucepan. Add 4 tablespoons of the dressing, cover and soften over a gentle heat for 2 minutes. Strain the sorrel or spinach and cool to room temperature.

5 Arrange the salmon, spring vegetables and potatoes on four large plates. Place a spoonful of sorrel or spinach on each piece of salmon, top with a halved hard-boiled quail's egg and serve.

Wild Rice & Turkey Salad

INGREDIENTS

1 cup wild rice
2 celery stalks, thinly sliced
3 scallions, chopped
1½ cups mushrooms, quartered
1 pound cooked turkey breast, diced
1 teaspoon fresh thyme leaves
½ cup French dressing, made with
walnut oil
2 dessert pears
¼ cup walnut pieces, toasted
salt
4 thyme sprigs, to garnish

SERVES 4

28

1 Bring a large saucepan of lightly salted water to a boil. Add the wild rice, bring back to a gentle boil and cook for 40–50 minutes, or until the rice is tender but still firm and the grains have begun to split. Drain well. When cool, tip into a bowl.

2 Add the celery, scallions, mushrooms, turkey and fresh thyme leaves to the bowl. Pour over the French dressing and toss together gently to coat thoroughly.

3 Cut the pears in half. Peel them and remove the cores, then thinly slice the halves lengthways without cutting through the stalk end. Spread the slices out like a fan.

4 Spoon the salad on to four plates, leaving a space on each for a fanned pear. Add the pears and walnuts and garnish with the thyme. Serve at once.

Swiss Cheese & Chicken Salad

INGREDIENTS

2 boned and skinned chicken breasts, cooked
8 ounces cooked ham or ox tongue, sliced
¼ inch thick
8 ounces Swiss cheese
1 crinkly green leaf lettuce, separated into leaves
1 butterhead lettuce, separated into leaves
1 bunch watercress, trimmed
3 celery stalks, thinly sliced
2 green-skinned eating apples
4 tablespoons sesame seeds, toasted
salt and ground black pepper
grated nutmeg
DRESSING
3 tablespoons lemon juice
2 teaspoons chopped fresh mint
3 drops of Tabasco sauce
5 tablespoons peanut or sunflower oil
1 teaspoon sesame oil

SERVES 4

1 Make the dressing. Mix the lemon juice, mint and Tabasco in a small bowl. Gradually whisk in the oils. Alternatively, mix all the ingredients in a screw-top jar, close tightly and shake to combine.

2 Slice the chicken, ham or tongue and cheese into fine strips. Place in a bowl, moisten with a little of the dressing and set aside.

3 Put the prepared lettuce leaves, watercress and celery in a separate bowl and gently mix together. Quarter and core the apples, then slice them directly into the bowl. Add the remaining dressing and toss lightly together until well coated.

4 Place the salad on four plates. Pile the meat and cheese strips in the center. Scatter with the sesame seeds, season with salt, pepper and nutmeg and serve.

Avocado, Crab & Cilantro Salad

INGREDIENTS

1½ pounds small new potatoes, scrubbed
1 mint sprig
*2-pound boiled crab or 10 ounces frozen
crabmeat, thawed*
*1 butterhead or escarole lettuce, separated
into leaves*
6 ounces corn salad or young spinach leaves
6 ounces cherry tomatoes
1 large ripe avocado
salt and ground black pepper
grated nutmeg
DRESSING
1 tablespoon freshly squeezed lime juice
3 tablespoons chopped fresh cilantro
½ teaspoon sugar
5 tablespoons olive oil

SERVES 4

1 Place the potatoes in a large saucepan of salted water. Add the mint. Bring to a boil, lower the heat slightly and cook for 15–20 minutes or until just tender. Drain, cover and keep warm until needed.

2 Lay the crab on its back and twist off the legs and claws where they join the body. Crack them open with the back of a chopping knife or lobster cracker and pick out the white meat with a skewer.

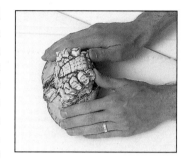

3 Hold the shell firmly and push the body section upwards, easing it out with your thumbs. Remove the flesh from inside the shell, then discard the grey feather-like gills. Crack the body section open and remove the white and dark flesh with a skewer.

4 Make the dressing. Mix the lime juice, cilantro and sugar in a small bowl. Gradually whisk in the oil. Alternatively, mix all the ingredients in a screw-top jar, close tightly and shake to combine. Toss the prepared salad leaves with a little of the dressing.

5 Place the salad on four large plates and distribute the cherry tomatoes among them. Cut the avocado in half and remove the pit and the skin. Slice thinly and arrange on the salads. Top the salads with the crab and distribute the warm new potatoes among them. Drizzle with the dressing, season with salt, pepper and nutmeg and serve.

Warm Salads

Wild Mushroom Salad with Prosciutto

INGREDIENTS

6 ounces prosciutto, thickly sliced
3 tablespoons butter
6½ cups wild and cultivated mushrooms, sliced
½ oakleaf lettuce, separated into leaves
½ frisée lettuce, separated into leaves
1 tablespoon walnut oil
4 tablespoons brandy
HERB CREPES
3 tablespoons flour
5 tablespoons milk
1 egg plus 1 egg yolk
4 tablespoons freshly grated Parmesan cheese
3 tablespoons chopped mixed fresh herbs
salt and ground black pepper

SERVES 4

1 Make the crêpes. Mix the flour and milk in a measuring cup. Beat in the egg, egg yolk, Parmesan and herbs. Add salt and pepper to taste. Place a lightly greased frying pan over a steady heat. Pour in enough mixture to coat the bottom of the pan.

2 When the batter has set, flip the crêpe over and cook the other side, then turn out. Cook more crêpes in the same way. When the crêpes are cool, roll them up together and slice into ribbons.

3 Cut the prosciutto into strips to match the crêpe ribbons and toss them lightly together in a bowl. Heat the butter in the clean frying pan. Add the mushrooms and cook for 6–8 minutes.

4 Meanwhile dress the prepared salad greens with walnut oil. Divide them among four large plates and arrange the prosciutto and crêpe ribbons in the center of each one. Add the brandy to the mushrooms and ignite it. As soon as the flames die down, spoon the mushrooms over the salads. Season with salt and pepper, and serve.

33

Warm Duck Salad with Orange & Coriander

Ingredients

1 small orange
2 boned duck breasts
²⁄₃ cup dry white wine
1 teaspoon ground coriander
½ teaspoon ground cumin
2 tablespoons sugar
juice of ½ lime or small lemon
½ escarole lettuce, separated into leaves
½ frisée lettuce, separated into leaves
2 tablespoons sunflower oil
salt and cayenne pepper
4 cilantro sprigs, to garnish
GARLIC CROUTONS
1 garlic clove
3 tablespoons olive oil
3 thick slices day-old bread,
cut into short fingers

SERVES 4

1 Cut the orange in half, then into thick slices. Discard any pips and place the slices in a small saucepan. Add water to cover, heat to simmering and cook for 5 minutes. Drain and set aside.

2 Prick the skin on the duck breasts, then rub the skin with salt. Heat a heavy-bottomed frying pan, add the duck breasts and cook for 20 minutes, turning once, until they are medium-rare.

3 Transfer the duck breasts to a heated plate, cover and keep hot. Pour off the fat from the pan, leaving the sediment behind.

4 Add the wine, spices and sugar to the frying pan and stir over the heat, taking care to incorporate the sediment. Add the orange slices. Boil quickly until the sauce coats the oranges, then sharpen with the lime or lemon juice. Add salt and cayenne to taste and keep warm over a low heat.

5 Make the croûtons in a second frying pan. Peel and bruise the garlic clove. Heat the olive oil with the garlic and when the garlic turns a deep golden brown, remove it with a slotted spoon. Add the bread fingers to the pan and fry until golden brown. Remove and drain on paper towels.

6 Sprinkle the prepared salad greens with the sunflower oil and arrange on four large plates. Cut the duck breasts into thick slices diagonally. Using the composition illustrated opposite, or one of your own, add the duck and glazed orange slices to the plates. Scatter with the croûtons, garnish each salad with a cilantro sprig and serve.

34

Spinach & Bacon Salad

INGREDIENTS

*1 pound young spinach, leaves stripped
from stems
4 tablespoons red wine vinegar
4 tablespoons water
4 teaspoons sugar
1 teaspoon dry mustard
1½ tablespoons sunflower oil
8 ounces rindless bacon strips
8 scallions, thinly sliced
6 radishes, thinly sliced
2 hard-boiled eggs, coarsely grated
salt and ground black pepper*

SERVES 6

1 Put the prepared spinach leaves in a large salad bowl. Mix the vinegar, water, sugar and dry mustard in a separate bowl. Add a pinch of salt and a grinding of black pepper.

2 Heat the oil in a frying pan, add the bacon strips and fry until very crisp and brown. Remove them with tongs and drain them well on kitchen paper.

3 Add the vinegar mixture to the bacon fat remaining in the pan. Bring to a boil, stirring constantly to incorporate any sediment on the base of the pan. Immediately pour the hot dressing over the spinach salad. Toss quickly to coat the leaves well.

4 Chop the bacon roughly and add it to the spinach. Add the scallions and radishes and mix gently. Scatter the grated hard-boiled egg over the salad, season to taste and serve at once.

Green Lentil & Cabbage Salad

INGREDIENTS

1 cup Puy or green lentils, soaked in cold water
to cover for 2 hours
2½ cups water
3 garlic cloves
1 bay leaf
1 small onion, peeled and studded with 2 cloves
1 tablespoon olive oil
1 red onion, thinly sliced
1 tablespoon thyme leaves
12 ounces cabbage, finely shredded
finely grated rind and juice of 1 lemon
1 tablespoon raspberry or red wine vinegar
salt and ground black pepper

SERVES 4–6

37

1 Drain the lentils and place them in a large saucepan. Pour over the water. Peel one garlic clove, leaving it whole, and add it to the saucepan with the bay leaf and studded onion. Bring to a boil and cook over a high heat for 10 minutes. Lower the heat, cover and cook for 25–35 minutes or until the lentils are tender. Remove the bay leaf and onion.

2 Meanwhile gently heat the oil in a large pan. Peel and crush the remaining garlic cloves and add them to the pan with the red onion and thyme. Cook for 10 minutes or until the onion is soft.

3 Add the cabbage, raise the heat and cook for 3–5 minutes, until just cooked but still crunchy. Drain the lentils if necessary and add them to the pan with the lemon rind and juice, and the vinegar.

4 Season the warm salad generously with salt and pepper, spoon into a bowl and serve at once with warm crusty French bread, if liked.

Mussel & Lentil Salad

INGREDIENTS

4 tablespoons olive oil
1 onion, finely chopped
1½ cups Puy or green lentils, soaked in cold
water to cover for 2 hours
3¾ cups vegetable broth
2 large carrots, cut into matchsticks
4 celery stalks, cut into matchsticks
2 pounds young spinach, leaves stripped
from stems
1 garlic clove, halved
4½ pounds live mussels, scrubbed and bearded
5 tablespoons white wine
generous pinch of saffron strands
½ teaspoon mild curry paste
2 tablespoons heavy cream
salt and cayenne pepper

SERVES 4

1 Heat 3 tablespoons of the oil in a saucepan and cook the onion on a low heat for 10 minutes. Add the drained lentils and broth to the pan. Bring to a boil and cook for 10 minutes. Lower the heat, cover and cook for 25–35 minutes until tender.

2 Meanwhile bring a small pan of water to a boil. Cook the carrot and celery matchsticks for about 3 minutes. Drain, cool, put in a bowl and moisten with some of the remaining oil.

3 Rinse the spinach leaves and place in a clean pan. Cover tightly, steam for 30 seconds, then refresh under cold water. Drain well, pressing the leaves gently against the sides of the colander or strainer to extract the excess liquid. Rub the cut clove of garlic thoroughly around the inside of a bowl, tip in the spinach and toss with the remaining oil.

4 Discard any mussels which do not close when tapped. Place the rest in a large saucepan. Add the wine, cover and cook over a high heat for 5–8 minutes, shaking the pan frequently, until the mussels have opened. Discard any that remain closed. Drain, reserving the cooking liquid. When cool, remove all but 4 of the mussels from their shells.

5 Strain the mussel liquid through a fine strainer into a deep frying pan. Stir in the saffron strands and leave to soak for 5 minutes, then stir in the curry paste. Cook over a high heat until most of the liquid has evaporated. Remove from the heat, stir in the cream and add the shelled mussels, with salt and cayenne to taste. Toss to coat.

6 Drain the lentils if necessary and spoon them into the center of four large plates. Surround each mound of lentils with five tiny heaps of spinach. Arrange a few carrot and celery matchsticks on top of each spinach portion. Spoon the mussels and sauce over the lentils. Garnish each plate with an opened mussel in the shell and serve warm.

Side Salads

Lettuce & Herb Salad

Ingredients

½ cucumber
mixed salad leaves
1 bunch watercress, trimmed
1 head Belgian endive, sliced
3 tablespoons chopped mixed fresh herbs
(parsley, thyme, mint, tarragon and chives)
Dressing
1 tablespoon wine vinegar
1 teaspoon mustard
5 tablespoons olive oil
salt and ground black pepper

Serves 4

1 Make the dressing. Put the wine vinegar and mustard in a small bowl and mix together. Whisk in the olive oil gradually and then add salt and pepper to taste. Alternatively, mix all the ingredients in a screw-top jar, close tightly and shake to combine.

2 Peel the cucumber, if liked, then halve it lengthwise and scoop out the seeds. Thinly slice the flesh. Tear the prepared mixed salad leaves into bite-size pieces.

3 Mix together the cucumber, salad leaves, watercress, Belgian endive and fresh herbs in a large bowl. Add the dressing and toss to coat. Serve the salad at once.

Apple & Date Coleslaw

INGREDIENTS

1 dessert pear
1 red-skinned eating apple
8 ounces red or white cabbage, or a mixture
3 carrots
7-ounce can flageolet or kidney beans, drained
⅓ cup chopped dates
DRESSING
½ teaspoon dry mustard
2 teaspoons clear honey
2 tablespoons orange juice
1 teaspoon white wine vinegar
½ teaspoon paprika
salt and ground black pepper

SERVES 4–6

1 Make the dressing. In a small bowl, mix the mustard and honey until smooth. Add the orange juice, vinegar, paprika, salt and pepper to taste. Mix well.

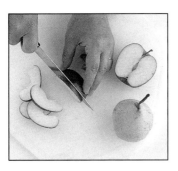

2 Cut the pear and apple into quarters, leaving the skin on. Remove the cores and slice the fruit thinly. Place in a bowl and toss with a little of the dressing.

3 Cut away the core from the cabbage. Shred the cabbage leaves very finely, discarding any other tough portions. Cut the carrots into very thin

strips, about 2 inches long. Add the cabbage, carrots, beans and dates to the bowl. Mix well.

4 Pour all the remaining dressing over the coleslaw and toss thoroughly to coat. Cover and refrigerate for about 30 minutes before serving.

COOK'S TIP
White raisins can be used instead of dates, if preferred. Leave to marinate in the dressing for 15 minutes. Add the dressing and white raisins to the coleslaw and mix well.

Tomato & Feta Cheese Salad

INGREDIENTS

2 pounds ripe tomatoes
7 ounces feta cheese
½ cup extra virgin olive oil
12 black olives
ground black pepper
4 basil sprigs, to garnish (optional)

SERVES 4

44

1 Using a small, pointed knife cut around and then remove the tough cores from the tomatoes. Cut the tomatoes in thick slices and arrange in a shallow dish.

2 Crumble the feta cheese over the sliced tomatoes. Drizzle over the oil, add the olives and a grinding of black pepper. Garnish with the basil, if liked.

COOK'S TIP

It is traditional to use only olive oil when dressing tomato salads, but a dash of balsamic vinegar may be added to the oil if the tomatoes are particularly sweet, or if this is more to your taste.

Marinated Cucumber Salad

INGREDIENTS

2 cucumbers
1 tablespoon salt
scant ½ cup sugar
¾ cup hard cider
1 tablespoon cider vinegar
3 tablespoons chopped fresh dill
ground black pepper

SERVES 4–6

45

1 Slice the cucumbers thinly and spread them in a colander, sprinkling salt between each layer. Set the colander over a bowl and leave to drain for 1 hour.

2 Meanwhile, mix the sugar, cider and cider vinegar in a saucepan. Heat gently, stirring all the time until the sugar has all dissolved. Leave to become cold.

3 Rinse all the cucumber slices very thoroughly under cold running water to remove the excess salt, then pat dry on paper towels and place in a

bowl. Pour over the cold cider mixture, cover and leave to marinate for 2 hours.

4 Drain the cucumber and sprinkle with the fresh dill and black pepper to taste. Transfer to a serving dish. Mix well, cover and chill until ready to serve.

Coronation Salad

INGREDIENTS

1 pound new potatoes, scrubbed
3 tablespoons French dressing
3 scallions, chopped
6 hard-boiled eggs, halved
1 frisée lettuce, separated into leaves
*¼ cucumber, sliced, then cut into
very fine matchsticks*
6 large radishes, sliced
salad cress
salt and ground black pepper
CURRY DRESSING
2 tablespoons olive oil
1 small onion, finely chopped
*1 tablespoon mild curry powder or
korma spice mix*
2 teaspoons tomato paste
2 tablespoons lemon juice
2 tablespoons sherry
1 ¼ cups mayonnaise
⅔ cup plain yogurt

SERVES 6

1 Place the potatoes in a large saucepan of salted water. Bring to a boil, lower the heat slightly and cook for 15–20 minutes or until just tender. Drain the potatoes and tip them into a bowl. Add the French dressing and toss gently together until well coated. Set aside to cool.

2 Make the curry dressing. Heat the oil in a saucepan. Add the onion and fry for 5 minutes. Stir in the curry powder or spice mix and fry for a further 1 minute, then remove from the heat and add all the remaining dressing ingredients. Mix well.

3 Add the curry dressing and scallions to the potatoes, and season to taste. Add the hard-boiled eggs and mix lightly, taking care not to break them up. Cover and chill until ready to serve.

4 Line a serving platter with the prepared lettuce leaves and pile the salad in the center. Arrange the cucumber, radishes and snipped salad cress on top. Serve at once.

Pasta & Beet Salad

INGREDIENTS

2 uncooked beets, scrubbed
2 cups dried pasta shells or twists
3 tablespoons French dressing
2 celery stalks, thinly sliced
3 scallions, sliced
¾ cup walnuts or hazelnuts,
coarsely chopped
1 eating apple
1 frisée lettuce, separated into leaves
3 hard-boiled eggs, chopped
2 avocados
salt and ground black pepper
chopped salad cress, to garnish
HORSERADISH DRESSING
4 tablespoons mayonnaise
3 tablespoons plain yogurt
2 tablespoons milk
2 teaspoons horseradish cream

SERVES 8

1 Put the beets in a large pan of salted water. Bring to a boil, lower the heat slightly and cook for 45–55 minutes or until just tender. Drain, rub off the skins and leave to cool. Once cold, cut the beets into neat dice.

2 Make the horseradish dressing by mixing all the ingredients in a bowl.

3 Bring a large saucepan of lightly salted water to a boil. Add the pasta and cook for 10–12 minutes, until *al dente.* Drain, tip into a bowl and toss with the French dressing. Season to taste.

4 Add the beets, celery, scallions and nuts to the pasta. Core and thinly slice the apple and add it to the pasta mixture. Spoon the horseradish dressing over the top and mix well. Cover and chill.

5 Line a salad bowl with the prepared lettuce leaves. Pile the salad into the center and scatter over the chopped egg. Peel, pit and slice the avocados and arrange on top. Garnish with the salad cress.

Leeks with Parsley, Egg & Walnut Dressing

INGREDIENTS

1½ pounds young leeks, trimmed
1 hard-boiled egg
sprig of parsley, to garnish
DRESSING
4 tablespoons fresh parsley
2 tablespoons olive oil
juice of ½ lemon
½ cup walnut pieces, toasted
6 tablespoons water
1 teaspoon sugar
salt and ground black pepper

SERVES 4

1 Cut the trimmed leeks into 4-inch lengths, then rinse very well in cold water. Bring a saucepan of lightly salted water to a boil. Add the leeks to the saucepan and cook for 8 minutes. Drain, refresh under cold running water and drain again.

2 Make the dressing. Chop the parsley finely in a food processor or blender. Add the olive oil, lemon juice and walnuts and process until smooth. Mix in enough of the water to give a coating consistency, then add the sugar, with salt and pepper to taste.

3 Arrange the leeks on a serving platter. Spoon the sauce over. Finely grate the hard-boiled egg over the sauce and serve garnished with a sprig of parsley.

COOK'S TIP
This recipe can also be made using fresh seasonal vegetables, such as green asparagus tips or baby zucchini, in place of the leeks. Cook only until just tender.

Green Salad with Orange & Avocado

INGREDIENTS

2 seedless oranges
3 tablespoons lemon juice
1 teaspoon Dijon mustard
pinch of sugar
6 tablespoons olive oil
1 tablespoon walnut oil
1 leaf lettuce, separated into leaves
1 small bunch watercress, trimmed
a few frisée lettuce leaves
1 small bunch arugula, trimmed
1 red onion, thinly sliced in rings
1 avocado
½ cup walnut pieces, toasted
salt and ground black pepper

SERVES 4

1 Grate the rind from 1 orange and set it aside. Placing each orange in turn on a board, slice off the top and bottom neatly, taking care to remove all the pith. Using the same knife, cut off the peel on the sides of the orange, following the contours of the fruit. Then, holding the fruit over a bowl to catch the juice, slice carefully between the membranes to remove the segments.

2 Add the grated orange rind, lemon juice, mustard and sugar to 2 tablespoons of the orange juice. Gradually whisk in the oils, then add salt and pepper to taste. Alternatively, mix all the ingredients in a screw-top jar, close tightly and shake to combine.

3 Place the prepared salad greens in a bowl with the onion rings and orange segments. Cut the avocado in half, remove the pit and peel off the skin. Cut the flesh into cubes and add them to the bowl.

4 Pour over the orange dressing, toss gently to coat, scatter the walnuts on top and serve.

Watercress & Potato Salad

Ingredients

1 pound small new potatoes, scrubbed
1 bunch watercress, trimmed
7 ounces cherry tomatoes, halved
2 tablespoons pumpkin seeds
Dressing
3 tablespoons plain yogurt
1 tablespoon cider vinegar
1 teaspoon light brown sugar
salt and paprika

Serves 4

1 Put the potatoes in a large saucepan of salted water. Bring to a boil, lower the heat slightly and cook for 15–20 minutes or until just tender. Drain and cool.

2 Meanwhile make the dressing. Put the yogurt, cider vinegar, sugar, and salt and paprika to taste, into a small bowl. Using a small hand whisk, beat together until well combined. Alternatively, mix all the dressing ingredients in a screw-top jar, close tightly and shake vigorously to combine.

3 Mix the potatoes, watercress, tomatoes and pumpkin seeds in a salad bowl. Pour over the dressing and serve at once.

51

Cook's Tip

For a variation on this salad try using a mixture of watercress and baby spinach or arugula leaves and replace the pumpkin seeds with sunflower seeds or toasted pine nuts.

Classic Salads

Chef's Salad

INGREDIENTS

1 pound small new potatoes, scrubbed
1 crisphead or leaf lettuce, or 1 head Belgian
endive, separated into leaves
2 carrots, coarsely grated
½ small fennel bulb or 2 celery stalks,
finely sliced
¾ cup small mushrooms, sliced
¼ cucumber, chopped
1 small green or red bell pepper, seeded, cut in
half and sliced
4 tablespoons cooked peas or snow peas
1 cup mixed cooked lentils, red kidney beans,
and lima beans
2-3 hard-boiled eggs, quartered
salt and ground black pepper
salad cress, to garnish
DRESSING
4 tablespoons mayonnaise
3 tablespoons plain yogurt
2 tablespoons milk
2 tablespoons snipped chives

SERVES 6

1 Place the potatoes in a large saucepan of salted water. Bring to a boil, lower the heat slightly and cook for 15–20 minutes or until just tender. Drain and leave to cool.

2 Make the dressing. Put all the dressing ingredients in a small bowl and mix together well with a fork or hand whisk. Add salt and pepper to taste.

3 Line a large serving platter with the prepared salad greens. Mix the potatoes with all the other vegetables, lentils and beans in a large bowl. Add salt and pepper to taste. Pour the dressing over the salad and toss together thoroughly.

4 Spoon the potato mixture onto the lettuce or Belgian endive leaves, top with the eggs and garnish with snipped cress. Serve lightly chilled.

Salade Niçoise

INGREDIENTS

1½ pounds potatoes, peeled
8 ounces green beans, topped and tailed
8 ounces small plum tomatoes, quartered,
or cherry tomatoes
1 cup French dressing
1 romaine lettuce, separated into leaves
14-ounce can tuna in oil,
drained and broken into large flakes
3 hard-boiled eggs, quartered
2-ounce can anchovy fillets, drained
2 tablespoons rinsed capers
12 black olives
salt and ground black pepper

SERVES 4

1 Place the potatoes in a large saucepan of salted water. Bring to a boil, lower the heat slightly and cook for 15–20 minutes. Drain, cool under cold running water and drain again. Slice thickly.

2 Cook the beans in a second pan of boiling water for 6 minutes. Drain, refresh under cold running water and drain again.

3 Mix together the potato slices, beans and plum or cherry tomatoes in a bowl. Add half of the French dressing and toss gently together until well coated.

4 Chop or tear the prepared salad greens roughly and place them in a large salad bowl. Pour the rest of the French dress-ing over the salad greens and toss together very lightly. Add the potato slices, beans and tomatoes to the dressed greens and divide among individual serving plates.

5 Distribute the flaked tuna over the salads with the hard-boiled egg quarters, anchovy fillets, capers and olives, pitted if liked. Season to taste and serve the salads at once.

Caesar Salad

INGREDIENTS

2 thick slices of bread, crusts removed
3 tablespoons sunflower oil
2 whole garlic cloves, peeled
1 romaine lettuce, separated into leaves
½ cup freshly grated Parmesan cheese
DRESSING
2 eggs
2 teaspoons Dijon mustard
2 teaspoons Worcestershire sauce
2 tablespoons lemon juice
3 tablespoons extra virgin olive oil

SERVES 4

1 Preheat the oven to 375°F. Cut the bread into cubes. Heat the oil gently in a saucepan. Add one of the garlic cloves and cook until golden. Remove the garlic, then add the bread cubes and toss to coat in the flavored oil.

2 Spread out the garlic-flavored bread cubes on a baking sheet. Bake in the oven for 10–12 minutes until golden and crisp. Leave to cool.

3 Cut the remaining garlic clove in half. Rub the cut sides around the inside of a large salad bowl. Tear the prepared salad greens into pieces and toss them into the bowl, sprinkling Parmesan cheese between the layers. Cover the salad and set aside.

4 Make the dressing. Bring a small saucepan of water to a boil. Add the eggs and cook for 1 minute only. Remove with a slotted spoon. Crack the eggs into a measuring cup or bowl. The whites should be milky and the yolks raw.

5 Add the remaining dressing ingredients to the eggs and whisk well. To serve, pour the dressing over the leaves, toss well and top with the croûtons.

COOK'S TIP
As the eggs for the dressing are barely cooked they must be perfectly fresh and bought from a reputable supplier, and the dressing should be made only just before serving.

Waldorf Ham Salad

INGREDIENTS

3 eating apples
1 tablespoon lemon juice
2 slices of cooked ham, about 6 ounces each
3 celery stalks
⅔ cup mayonnaise
½ bunch watercress, trimmed
1 escarole lettuce, separated into leaves
1 small radicchio, separated into leaves
3 tablespoons walnut oil or olive oil
½ cup walnut pieces, toasted
salt and ground black pepper

SERVES 4

1 Quarter, peel and core the apples. Cut them into fine shreds, put in a bowl and toss with the lemon juice to prevent them turning brown.

2 Cut the ham and celery into 2-inch strips and add to the apples. Spoon the mayonnaise over the apple, ham and celery mixture and toss to coat.

3 Slice the prepared escarole and radicchio leaves into fine shreds, put in a bowl and toss with the oil. Either set aside the watercress sprigs for garnishing or toss them with the lettuce now. Divide the dressed leaves among four plates.

4 Pile the mayonnaise mixture in the center of each bed of leaves. Season with salt and pepper. Scatter the toasted walnuts on top and serve the salads at once, garnished with the watercress sprigs, if these have not yet been used.

Russian Salad

INGREDIENTS

1½ cups mushrooms
12 ounces cooked shrimp, peeled and deveined
1 large gherkin, chopped, or 2 tablespoons rinsed capers
½ cup mayonnaise
1 tablespoon lemon juice
4 ounces small new potatoes, scrubbed
4 ounces young carrots
4 ounces baby corn cobs
4 ounces baby turnips, trimmed
½ cup fava beans
1 tablespoon olive oil
4 hard-boiled eggs
salt and ground black pepper
½ x 2-ounce can anchovy fillets, drained and cut into fine strips, and paprika, to garnish

SERVES 4

1 Slice the mushrooms thinly and cut into matchsticks. Put in a bowl with the shrimp and gherkin or capers. Mix the mayonnaise and lemon juice in a small bowl and fold half into the mushroom mixture. Add salt and pepper to taste and mix gently.

2 Place the potatoes in a large saucepan of salted water. Bring to a boil, lower the heat slightly and cook for 15–20 minutes or until just tender.

3 Cook the carrots, corn and turnips in a separate pan of salted, boiling water for 6 minutes.

4 Bring another pan of salted water to a boil. Add the fava beans and cook for 3 minutes. Drain and refresh under cold water. Pinch each bean between your fingers to pop off the skins, revealing a tender green bean. Discard the skins.

5 Drain the potatoes and other vegetables, cool them under cold running water and drain well. Tip into a bowl, moisten with olive oil, then divide among four salad bowls. Spoon on the skinned fava beans and dressed shrimp. Place a hard-boiled egg in the center of each salad, garnish with strips of anchovy and sprinkle with paprika.

Gado Gado

INGREDIENTS

2 potatoes, peeled
6 ounces green beans, trimmed
1 romaine lettuce, washed and trimmed
3 hard-boiled eggs, quartered
½ cucumber, peeled and cut into fingers
12 ounces large cooked shrimp tails
4 ounces bean sprouts
1 small daikon radish, peeled and grated
1 small bunch fresh cilantro
6 ounces bean curd, cut into large dice
4 tomatoes, cut into wedges
SPICY PEANUT SAUCE
2 shallots or 1 small onion, chopped
½ cup smooth peanut butter
juice of ½ lemon
1 garlic clove, crushed
2 small red chilies, seeded and finely chopped
2 tablespoons oriental fish
sauce (optional)
⅔ cup coconut milk,
canned or fresh
1 tablespoon sugar

SERVES 4

1 Make the peanut sauce. Put all the sauce ingredients into a food processor or blender and process until smooth. Scrape into a bowl and set aside.

2 Place the potatoes in a large saucepan of salted water. Bring to a boil, lower the heat slightly and cook for about 20 minutes or until just tender. Cook the beans in a separate pan of boiling water for 6 minutes. Drain the vegetables, refresh under cold running water and drain again. Leave to cool.

3 Use the outer leaves of the prepared romaine lettuce to line a large platter. Pile the remaining leaves to one side of the platter. Slice the potatoes. Arrange the potatoes, beans, hard-boiled eggs, cucumber, prawns, bean sprouts, radish, cilantro, bean curd and tomatoes in separate piles on the platter, leaving a space to accommodate the bowl of sauce.

4 Serve the salad lightly chilled with the peanut sauce in place. Guests make their own salad packages, wrapping the fillings of their choice in lettuce leaves and dipping them in the spicy peanut sauce.

Shrimp Salad with Curry Dressing

INGREDIENTS

1 ripe tomato
½ crisphead lettuce, shredded
1 small bunch fresh cilantro, finely chopped
1 small onion, finely chopped
1 tablespoon lemon juice
1 pound cooked shrimp, peeled and deveined
1 eating apple
salt

DRESSING

5 tablespoons mayonnaise
1 teaspoon mild curry paste
1 tablespoon tomato ketchup
2 tablespoons water

GARNISH

8 cooked shrimp, in the shell
8 lemon wedges
4 fresh cilantro sprigs

SERVES 4

1 Plunge the tomato into a saucepan of boiling water for 1 minute, then transfer it to a bowl of cold water. Slip off the skin, remove the core and seeds and cut the flesh into large dice.

2 Mix the lettuce, cilantro, tomato and onion in a bowl. Moisten with the lemon juice and add salt to taste. Divide the mixture among four salad plates or bowls.

3 Make the dressing. Mix the mayonnaise with the mild curry paste and ketchup in a small bowl. Stir in the water and add salt to taste. Mix with the peeled shrimp and stir to combine. Quarter and core the apple and coarsely grate it into the mixture.

4 Pile a quarter of the shrimp mixture onto each plate of salad, then garnish each with 2 whole shrimp, lemon wedges and finally a sprig of fresh cilantro.

Index